Famil
Histories

My
Caribbean
family history

Vic Parker

Heinemann
LIBRARY

Young
Explorer

www.heinemann.co.uk/library
Visit our website to find out more information about Heinemann Library books.

To order:
☎ Phone 44 (0) 1865 888066
▤ Send a fax to 44 (0) 1865 314091
▣ Visit the Heinemann Bookshop at www.heinemann.co.uk/library to browse our catalogue and order online.

First published in Great Britain by Heinemann Library, Halley Court, Jordan Hill, Oxford OX2 8EJ, part of Harcourt Education. Heinemann is a registered trademark of Harcourt Education Ltd.

Editorial: Charlotte Guillain
Design: Joanna Hinton-Malivoire
Picture research: Erica Martin
Production: Duncan Gilbert
Illustrated by Jacqueline McQuade
Originated by Modern Age

Printed and bound in China by South China Printing Co. Ltd.

ISBN 978 0 4310 1499 9 (hardback)
ISBN 978 0 4310 1504 0 (paperback)

12 11 10 09 08
10 9 8 7 6 5 4 3 2 1

British Library Cataloguing in Publication Data
Parker, Vic
My Caribbean family history. - (Family histories)
305.9'06912
A full catalogue record for this book is available from the British Library.

Acknowledgements
The publishers would like to thank the following for permission to reproduce photographs:
© Alamy pp. **24**, **27** (Vehbi Koca); © Anthony Blake Photo Library p. **19** (S Lee Studios); © Corbis pp. **8** (E.O. Hoppé), **20** (Homer Sykes), **21** (Comstock); © Mary Evans p. **14** (Roger Mayne); © Getty Images p. **17** (D. Baxter); © Images of Empire p. **7**; © Herbert Lewis p. **11** (Hulton Archive/Getty Images); © Popperfoto.com pp. **13**, **22**; © Topfoto p. **18** (The image works/Mel Rosenthal)

Cover photograph of child's face reproduced with permission of © Alamy (BananaStock).

Every effort has been made to contact copyright holders of any material reproduced in this book. Any omissions will be rectified in subsequent printings if notice is given to the publishers.

Disclaimer
All the Internet addresses (URLs) given in this book were valid at the time of going to press. However, due to the dynamic nature of the Internet, some addresses may have changed, or sites may have changed or ceased to exist since publication. While the author and publishers regret any inconvenience this may cause readers, no responsibility for any such changes can be accepted by either the author or publishers.

Contents

Words appearing in the text in bold, **like this**, are explained in the Glossary.

Joel's family history

My name is Joel. I am nine years old. I live with my mother, father, and sister in a city called Birmingham.

Birmingham is in the Midlands of England.

My family comes from the Caribbean. The Caribbean is a group of islands near North and South America. The weather is sunny and hot, but there is often heavy rain too. The islands have sandy beaches and some have mountains covered with steamy **rainforests**.

My family tree

My mother's parents

Desmond Williams
(my grandfather)
born 1925
Jamaica

Gloria Jackson
(my grandmother)
born 1927
Barbados

My father's parents

Dudley Riley
(my grandfather)
born 1924
Jamaica

Regina Stewart
(my grandmother)
born 1930
Jamaica

My grandparents grew up in the Caribbean. They came from two islands, Jamaica and Barbados. Jamaica and Barbados were ruled by Britain for over 300 years, so people there speak English.

My grandfather grew up in Kingston, the **capital** of Jamaica.

My grandfather Desmond lived in a big town in Jamaica called Kingston. In the countryside all around there were large sugar cane and banana farms. Kingston was an important centre for traders. The harbour was always busy with **merchants'** ships.

Bananas were sold to Britain and other countries in Europe.

My great-grandfather was a businessman. He made his money from a small banana farm. He also bought several houses in Kingston and rented them to people.

My grandfather lived with his four sisters and two brothers in a beautiful wooden house.

My grandfather's home in Kingston had electricity and running water. In the countryside, houses did not have these. His home had a **parlour**, a dining room, a bathroom, and three bedrooms. The kitchen was outside, because people worried that wooden houses might catch fire when they cooked things.

My grandfather's favourite toys were his wooden yoyo and cricket set. He played with toys and games that he made himself, like jacks, marbles, spinning tops, and hopscotch.

My grandfather's family never had many new things. Their clothes were handed down from older children.

Boys and girls were taught in separate schools. Everyone had to buy their own books and pens.

My grandfather worked hard at school. The teachers were very strict. If you were naughty, one punishment was to be hit with a cane.

In 1939, Britain and other European countries began fighting against Germany in **World War Two**. Britain asked people from other countries to help. In 1943, my grandfather was 18 years old. He went to Britain to train to be a mechanic in the army.

Great Britain

Germany

The Caribbean

Thousands of young men from the Caribbean went to Europe to fight in World War Two.

The journey from Jamaica to England took one month.

The war finished in 1945 and my grandfather went home to Jamaica. But Britain was very short of workers. Three years later, my grandfather returned to Britain to stay. He travelled with nearly 500 other Jamaican men on a ship called the SS *Empire Windrush*.

Britain seemed very cold and grey compared to the hot, bright Caribbean.

My grandfather went to work in Birmingham. He got a job sorting letters in the post office. He rented a small house with several other men from Jamaica.

Soon more people arrived from the Caribbean to live in Birmingham. My grandfather met a young woman called Gloria who had come from Barbados. She worked as a hospital nurse. They fell in love and got married.

My grandfather and grandmother rented a small house of their own. They saved up for **luxuries** like a fridge, a vacuum cleaner, and a washing machine. Like many people then, they could not afford their own television set or telephone for a long time. They had four children.

My family tree

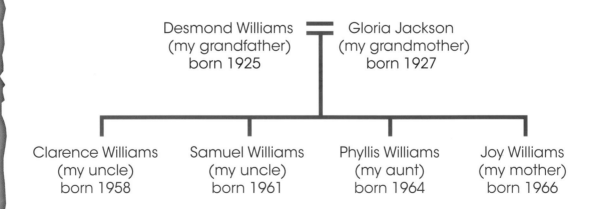

Desmond Williams
(my grandfather)
born 1925

Gloria Jackson
(my grandmother)
born 1927

Clarence Williams
(my uncle)
born 1958

Samuel Williams
(my uncle)
born 1961

Phyllis Williams
(my aunt)
born 1964

Joy Williams
(my mother)
born 1966

My mother grew up among several Caribbean neighbours.

My mother was the best in her class at maths and music. But she often felt different at school because most of the children were white. They sometimes made fun of her because her skin was a different colour and she said some words with a Caribbean **accent**.

Many Caribbean people are **Christians**.

Every Sunday, my grandparents took my mother and her brothers and sister to church. Lots of Caribbean people squashed into a small hall to pray. Everyone joined the **minister** singing and clapping along to the hymns.

My grandmother taught my mother how to cook tasty Caribbean food. She passed down all the recipes her own mother had taught her. The recipes were not written down, just remembered.

My mother's favourite meal was rice and peas, **plantain**, and chicken.

My mother enjoyed singing in a **gospel choir** when she was a teenager. She would take part in concerts as well as singing every week at church. Some of her best friends sang in the choir with her.

My mother dreamed of owning her own hair salon one day.

My mother decided she wanted to be a hairdresser. When she left school, she went to work in a **salon**. She also had to go to college one day a week to learn extra skills.

There were many big car factories in the Midlands.

One of the girls my mother worked with had a brother called Ray. Ray's family were from Jamaica too. Ray worked in a huge factory which made cars.

My mother and Ray fell in love and got married. They held a big wedding party in a special room at the car factory. They moved into a modern flat in a new block. They had three children.

My family tree

Ray Riley
(my father)
born 1968

Joy Williams
(my mother)
born 1966

Leon Riley
(my brother)
born 1991

Lola Riley
(my sister)
born 1991

Joel Riley
(me)
born 1997

At my school, there are lots of children whose families once came from the Caribbean. My favourite lesson is English. When I grow up I want to be a famous writer or maybe a teacher.

I took this photograph of my class assembly.

A Caribbean-style **steel band** plays at the carnival.

Every summer, my school holds a big Caribbean carnival. Everyone dresses up in costume. There is music and dancing and Caribbean food. My whole family comes along to enjoy themselves.

Then and now

My grandfather lived in a large wooden house with many brothers and sisters. I live in a small flat with one brother and one sister.

My grandfather's school was for boys only. They did not have many books. My school is for boys and girls. We have lots of books, equipment, and computers.

Joel's family tree

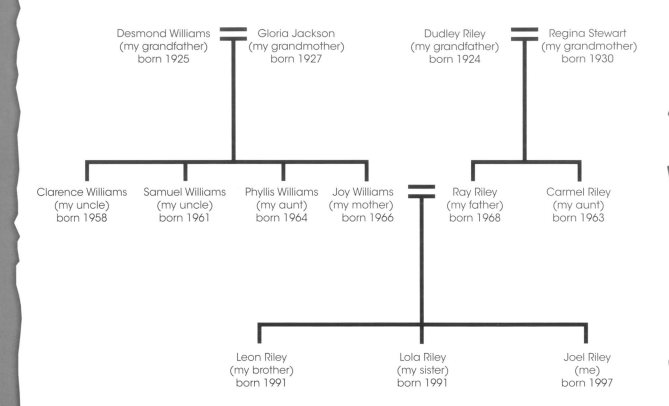

Desmond Williams
(my grandfather)
born 1925

Gloria Jackson
(my grandmother)
born 1927

Dudley Riley
(my grandfather)
born 1924

Regina Stewart
(my grandmother)
born 1930

Clarence Williams
(my uncle)
born 1958

Samuel Williams
(my uncle)
born 1961

Phyllis Williams
(my aunt)
born 1964

Joy Williams
(my mother)
born 1966

Ray Riley
(my father)
born 1968

Carmel Riley
(my aunt)
born 1963

Leon Riley
(my brother)
born 1991

Lola Riley
(my sister)
born 1991

Joel Riley
(me)
born 1997

Finding out about your family history

- See if your family members have any photographs of when they got married, or when they were young. You could turn the photographs into a family history scrapbook. Get your family to write their memories next to the photographs.

- Ask your family about what life was like when they grew up. What toys did they like to play with? What food did they like to eat? What were their friends like? Did they go through difficult times? You could record them talking or write down what they tell you.

- Ask your mother, father, aunts, uncles and grandparents to help you make your own family tree.

- Look at a map and draw circles around the places where your family has lived. Find out about those places using books and websites. See if your family can take you on trips there.

More books to read

Every Little Thing Will Be All Right, Diane Browne
(Carlong Publishers, 2003)

Traditional Tales from the Caribbean, Victoria Parker
(Belitha Press, 2001)

What's it like to live in Jamaica? Alison Brownlie
(Hodder Wayland, 2005)

Websites

www.bbc.co.uk/history/walk/memory_index.shtml
This website gives you tips on finding out about your
own family history.

http://pbskids.org/wayback/family/tree/index.html
This website helps you to put together your own
family tree.

Glossary

accent way people from a certain area pronounce words

capital city where a country's government is based

Christian person who follows the teachings of Jesus Christ in a book called the Bible

gospel choir group that sings Christian music in a particular style

luxuries something that you do not really need, just something that is nice to have

merchant person who buys and sells goods

minister person who leads a group of people in practising their religion

parlour living room kept neat and tidy for entertaining visitors

plantain vegetable which looks like a banana but which is not sweet

rainforest type of jungle found in hot, rainy places

salon shop where hairdressers work

steel band band that plays drums made from old oil barrels

World War Two war that many countries fought in, which took place from 1939 to 1945

Index